About Birds

A Guide for Children

Revised Edition

Cathryn Sill

Illustrated by John Sill

PEACHTREE

ATLANTA

For the One who created birds.

—*Genesis* 1:21

Published by
PEACHTREE PUBLISHING COMPANY INC.
1700 Chattahoochee Avenue
Atlanta, Georgia 30318-2112
www.peachtree-online.com

Text © 1991, 1997, 2013 by Cathryn P. Sill
Illustrations © 1991, 1997, 2013 by John C. Sill

Illustrations painted in watercolor on archival quality 100% rag watercolor paper
Text and titles set in Novarese from Adobe Systems
Edited by Vicky Holifield

Printed and manufactured in August 2019 in Stevens Point, WI by Worzalla in the
United States of America

10 9 8 7 6 5 4 3 2 (hardcover)
10 9 (trade paperback)
Revised edition

HC ISBN: 978-1-56145-688-8
PB ISBN: 978-1-56145-699-4

Library of Congress Cataloging-in-Publication Data

Sill, Cathryn P., 1953–
About birds / written by Cathryn P. Sill ; illustrated by John Sill.— 1st ed.
p. cm.
Summary: Text and illustrations introduce the world of birds from eggs to flight, from
songs to nests.
ISBN 1-56145-028-6
1. Birds—Juvenile literature. [1. Birds.] I. Sill, John, illus. II. Title.
QL676.2.S53   1991   91-16654
598—dc20   CIP
AC

About Birds

Birds have feathers.

Baby birds hatch from eggs.

Some birds build nests on the ground.

PLATE 3
Ovenbird

Some build in very high places.

PLATE 4
Bald Eagle

And some do not build a nest at all.

PLATE 5
Common Murre

Birds travel in different ways.

Most birds fly,

but some swim,

and others run.

Birds may flock together...

PLATE 10
Red-winged Blackbird

or live alone.

Birds use their bills to gather food.

a.

b.

c.

d.

e.

John Gill

They sing to let other birds know how they feel.

PLATE 13
Indigo Bunting

Birds come in all sizes.

Birds are important to us.

Afterword

PLATE 1

There are more than 10,000 species of birds in the world. Over 700 species live in the United States and Canada. Feathers protect birds from the elements. Because feathers are so light and strong, they enable birds to fly. Northern Cardinals are popular backyard birds in eastern areas of the U.S. and parts of the southwest. They live in brushy places with dense cover.

PLATE 2

Although all birds hatch from eggs, different species have different nesting habits. Female American Robins build cup-shaped nests in shrubs or trees from materials such as twigs, grass, feathers, and string. The nest is reinforced with soft mud and lined with fine grasses. American Robins are common across North America in many habitats, including fields, forests, shrub lands, tundra, and yards.

PLATE 3

Birds use nests to protect their eggs and chicks from predators and bad weather. Nests built on the ground are often hidden or camouflaged. Ovenbirds are named for their small dome-shaped nests that resemble old-fashioned ovens. These birds nest in forests across Canada and the eastern United States. In winter Ovenbirds migrate to the southeastern United States, the Caribbean, Mexico, Central America, and northern South America.

PLATE 4

Many birds build nests above the ground, varying the height according to the needs of individual species. Bald Eagles usually nest in tall trees that provide a wide view. They nest on cliff faces or even on the ground in areas where tall trees do not grow. Bald Eagles live in most of North America.

PLATE 5

Some birds scrape out a place to lay eggs right on the ground. Common Murres lay pointed pear-shaped eggs on rocky ledges. The elongated shape of the eggs causes them to roll in a circular motion, thus preventing them from toppling off the edge. Common Murres live on northern oceans around the world. They only come to shore to nest.

PLATE 6

Most birds use flight to move around. Flying helps them get food, find a safe place to raise young, and avoid predators. Canada Geese are strong flyers. They are able to migrate hundreds of miles in spring and fall. Canada Geese are native to most of North America. They have been introduced in England, northwest Europe, and New Zealand.

PLATE 7

Hummingbirds are able to fly forward, backward, sideways, and upside down. Ruby-throated Hummingbirds are powerful fliers, beating their wings about 53 times per second. They nest in eastern North America and migrate to Central America for the winter. Many of them fly across the Gulf of Mexico in a single flight.

PLATE 8

Some birds swim underwater to find food and avoid predators. Others stay on the surface most of the time. Wood Ducks have webbed feet that enable them to swim. They are also strong flyers. Wood Ducks live in wooded swamps and forested waterways across parts of North America and western Cuba.

PLATE 9

Birds that run spend much of their time on the ground. Most of them can also fly. Greater Roadrunners can run at speeds up to 18 mph (30 kph). They prefer running, but will fly to escape predators. Greater Roadrunners live in the southwestern United States and Mexico.

PLATE 10

Some birds flock together in fall and winter for protection. Red-winged Blackbirds often form huge flocks made up of thousands of birds. During the nesting season the flocks separate and each pair claims its own territory. Red-winged Blackbirds live in North and Central America.

PLATE 11

Many birds of prey are solitary except during the nesting season. Great Horned Owls live in different habitats across most of North America. They also live in parts of Central and South America.

PLATE 12

Birds' bills are shaped according to the food they eat. Birds also use their bills to preen their feathers, build nests, and defend themselves. Magnificent Hummingbirds live in the southwest United States and Central America. Evening Grosbeaks live in North America. Great Blue Herons and Cedar Waxwings live in North America, Central America, and northern parts of South America. Vermilion Flycatchers live in the southwestern United States, Central America, and South America.

PLATE 13

Birds use their voices to attract mates, defend their territory, and warn others of danger. Indigo Buntings are small songbirds that spend the summer in eastern and central North America. They migrate to Central America and the West Indies for the winter.

PLATE 14

Sizes of the illustrated birds:

a. Great Blue Heron—length 38" (96 cm), wingspan 70" (177 cm)
b. Bald Eagle—length 32" (81 cm), wingspan 80" (203 cm)
c. Great Horned Owl—length 20" (50 cm), wingspan 55" (139 cm)
d. Canada Goose—length 21½–43" (55–110 cm), wingspan 48–71½" (122–183 cm)
e. Wood Duck—length 13½" (34 cm), wingspan 28" (71 cm)
f. Northern Cardinal—length 7¾" (19.6 cm)
g. Red-winged Blackbird—length 7¼" (18 cm)
h. Indigo Bunting—length 4½" (11½ cm)
i. Ruby-throated Hummingbird—length 3¾" (9½ cm)

PLATE 15

Birds benefit human beings in many ways. They eat harmful insects, pollinate some flowers, disperse seeds, keep rodent populations down, and provide food for people. Observing birds brings great pleasure to people all over the world.

GLOSSARY

Camouflage—colors or patterns on an animal that help it hide
Migrate—to move periodically from one region to another
Predator—an animal that lives by hunting and eating other animals
Preen—to straighten or clean feathers
Species—a group of animals or plants that are alike in many ways

BIBLIOGRAPHY

BOOKS

BIRD (DK Eyewitness Books)
A PLACE FOR BIRDS by Melissa Stewart (Peachtree Publishers)
NATIONAL AUDUBON SOCIETY FIRST FIELD GUIDE: BIRDS by Scott Weidensaul (Scholastic, Inc.)
PETERSON FIRST GUIDES: BIRDS by Roger Tory Peterson (Houghton Mifflin Company)
THE YOUNG BIRDERS GUIDE TO BIRDS OF EASTERN NORTH AMERICA by Bill Thompson III (Houghton Mifflin Company)

WEBSITES

http://www.allaboutbirds.org/guide/search/ac
http://ibc.lynxeds.com/
http://animaldiversity.ummz.umich.edu./site/accounts/information/Aves.html

ABOUT... SERIES

ISBN 978-1-56145-234-7 HC
ISBN 978-1-56145-312-2 PB

ISBN 978-1-56145-038-1 HC
ISBN 978-1-56145-364-1 PB

ISBN 978-1-56145-688-8 HC
ISBN 978-1-56145-699-4 PB

ISBN 978-1-56145-301-6 HC
ISBN 978-1-56145-405-1 PB

ISBN 978-1-56145-256-9 HC
ISBN 978-1-56145-335-1 PB

ISBN 978-1-56145-588-1 HC

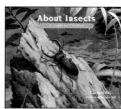

ISBN 978-1-56145-207-1 HC
ISBN 978-1-56145-232-3 PB

ISBN 978-1-56145-141-8 HC
ISBN 978-1-56145-174-6 PB

ISBN 978-1-56145-358-0 HC
ISBN 978-1-56145-407-5 PB

ISBN 978-1-56145-331-3 HC
ISBN 978-1-56145-406-8 PB

ISBN 978-1-56145-743-4 HC
ISBN 978-1-56145-741-0 PB

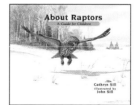

ISBN 978-1-56145-536-2 HC

ISBN 978-1-56145-183-8 HC
ISBN 978-1-56145-233-0 PB

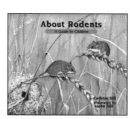

ISBN 978-1-56145-454-9 HC

ABOUT HABITATS SERIES

Deserts

ISBN 978-1-56145-641-3 HC
ISBN 978-1-56145-639-9 PB

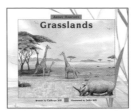

Grasslands

ISBN 978-1-56145-559-1 HC

Mountains

ISBN 978-1-56145-469-3 HC
ISBN 978-1-56145-731-1 PB

Wetlands

ISBN 978-1-56145-432-7 HC
ISBN 978-1-56145-689-5 PB

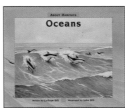

Oceans

ISBN 978-1-56145-618-5 HC

Forests

ISBN 978-1-56145-734-2 HC

THE SILLS

Cathryn Sill, a former elementary school teacher, is the author of the acclaimed ABOUT… series. With her husband John and her brother-in-law Ben Sill, she coauthored the popular bird-guide parodies, A FIELD GUIDE TO LITTLE-KNOWN AND SELDOM-SEEN BIRDS OF NORTH AMERICA, ANOTHER FIELD GUIDE TO LITTLE-KNOWN AND SELDOM-SEEN BIRDS OF NORTH AMERICA, and BEYOND BIRDWATCHING.

John Sill is a prize-winning and widely published wildlife artist who illustrated the ABOUT… series and illustrated and coauthored the FIELD GUIDES and BEYOND BIRDWATCHING. A native of North Carolina, he holds a B.S. in Wildlife Biology from North Carolina State University.

The Sills live in Franklin, North Carolina.